Marcus Eli Ravage

A Real Case Against the Jews

One of them points out the full depth of their guilt

OCR - Edition
LENCULUS
Exegi monumentum aere perennius

April 2018

Marcus Eli Ravage

Written by a Jewish author
and originally published in
The Century Magazine
in January 1928.

This article asserts that if
Whites understood the depths
to which Jews control our countries
and their institutions of power and
the way in which they wield that
power in an effort to destroy our
interests, we would rise-up
and eradicate them immediately.

OF COURSE, YOU DO RESENT US. It is no good telling me you don't. So let us not waste any time on denials and alibis. You know you do, and I know it, and we understand each other. To be sure, some of your best friends are Jews, and all that.

I have heard that before once or twice, I think. And I know, too, that you do not include me personally — "me" being any particular individual Jew — when you fling out at us in your wholesale fashion, because I am, well, so different, don't you know, almost as good as one of yourselves.

That little exemption does not, somehow, move me to gratitude; but never mind that now. It is the aggressive, climbing, pushing, materialistic sort you dislike — those, in a word, who remind you so much of your own up-and-coming brethren.

We understand each other perfectly. I don't hold it against you.

Bless my soul, I do not blame anybody for disliking anybody. The thing that intrigues me about this anti-Jewish business, as you play at it, is your total lack of grit.

You are so indirect and round-about with it, you make such fantastic and transparent excuses, you seem to be suffering from selfconsciousness so horribly, that if the performance were not grotesque it would be irritating.

It is not as if you were amateurs : you have been at it for over fifteen centuries. Yet watching you and hearing your childish pretexts, one might get the impression that you did not know yourselves what it is all about. You resent us, but you cannot clearly say why. You think up a new excuse — a "reason" is what you call it — every other day.

You have been piling up justifications for yourselves these many hundreds of years and each new invention is more laughable than the last and each new excuse contradicts and annihilates the last.

Not so many years ago I used to hear that we were money-grubbers and commercial materialists; now the complaint is being whispered around that no art and no profession is safe against Jewish invasion.

We are, if you are to be believed, at once clannish and exclusive and unassimilable because we won't intermarry with you, and we are also climbers and pushers and a menace to your racial integrity.

Our standard of living is so low that we create your slums and sweated industries, and so high that we crowd you out of your best residential sections.

We shirk our patriotic duty in wartime

because we are pacifists by nature and tradition, and we are the arch-plotters of universal wars and the chief beneficiaries of those wars (see the late "Dearborn Independent," *passim*, and "The Protocols of the Elders of Zion").

We are at once the founders and leading adherents of capitalism and the chief perpetrators of the rebellion against capitalism.

Surely, history has nothing like us for versatility!

And, oh! I almost forgot the reason of reasons. We are the stiff-necked people who never accepted Christianity, and we are the criminal people who crucified its founder.

But I tell you, you are self-deceivers. You lack either the self-knowledge or the mettle to face the facts squarely and own up to the truth. You resent the Jew not because, as some of you seem to think, he crucified Jesus but because he gave him birth. Your real quarrel with us is not that we have rejected Christianity but that we have imposed it upon you!

Your loose, contradictory charges against us are not a patch on the blackness of our proved historic offense. You accuse us of stirring up revolution in Moscow. Suppose we admit the charge. What of it?
Compared with what Paul the Jew of Tarsus accomplished in Rome, the Russian upheaval is a mere street brawl.

You make much noise and fury about the undue Jewish influence in your theaters and movie palaces. Very good; granted your complaint is well-founded. But what is that compared to our staggering influence in your churches, your schools, your laws and your governments, and the very thoughts you think every day ?

A clumsy Russian forges a set of papers and publishes them in a book called "The Protocols of the Elders of Zion," which shows that we plotted to bring on the late World War. You believe that book: All right. For the sake of argument we will underwrite every word of it. It is genuine and authentic. But what is that beside the unquestionable historical conspiracy which we have carried out, which we have never denied because you never had the courage to charge us with it, and of which the full record is extant for anybody to read ?

If you really are serious when you talk of Jewish plots, may I not direct your attention to one worth talking about ? What use is it wasting words on the alleged control of your public opinion by Jewish financiers, newspaper owners and movie magnates, when you might as well justly accuse us of the proved control of your whole civilization by the Jewish Gospels ?

You have not begun to appreciate the real depth of our guilt. We *are* intruders. We *are* disturbers. We *are* subverters. We have taken your natural world, your ideals, your destiny, and played havoc with them. We have been at the bottom not merely of the latest great war but of nearly all your wars, not only of the Russian but of every other major revolution in your history. We have brought discord and confusion and frustration into your personal and public life. We are still doing it. No one can tell how long we shall go on doing it.

Look back a little and see what has happened. Nineteen hundred years ago you were an innocent, carefree, pagan race. You worshipped countless gods and goddesses, the spirits of the air, of the running streams and of the woodland. You took unblushing pride in the glory of your naked bodies.
You carved images of your gods and of the tantalizing human figure. You delighted in the combats of the field, the arena and the battle-ground. War and slavery were fixed institutions in your systems. Disporting yourselves on the hillsides and in the valleys of the great outdoors, you took to speculating on the wonder and mystery of life and laid the foundations of natural science and philosophy. Yours was a noble, sensual culture, unirked by the prickings of a social conscience or by any sentimental questionings about

human equality. Who knows what great and glorious destiny might have been yours if we had left you alone.

But we did not leave you alone. We took you in hand and pulled down the beautiful and generous structure you had reared, and changed the whole course of your history. We conquered you as no empire of yours ever subjugated Africa or Asia. And we did it all without armies, without bullets, without blood or turmoil, without force of any kind. We did it solely by the irresistible might of our spirit, with ideas, with propaganda. We made you the willing and unconscious bearers of our mission to the whole world, to the barbarous races of the earth, to the countless unborn generations. Without fully understanding what we were doing to you, you became the agents at large of our racial tradition, carrying our gospel to the unexplored ends of the earth.

Our tribal customs have become the core of your moral code. Our tribal laws have furnished the basic groundwork of all your august constitutions and legal systems.

Our legends and our folk-tales are the sacred lore which you croon to your infants. Our poets have filled your hymnals and your prayer-books. Our national history has become an indispensable part of the learning of your pastors and priests and scholars. Our kings, our statesmen, our prophets, our warriors are your heroes. Our ancient little country is your Holy Land. Our national literature is your Holy Bible.
What our people thought and taught has become inextricably woven into your very speech and tradition, until no one among you can be called educated who is not familiar with our racial heritage.

Jewish artisans and Jewish fishermen are your teachers and your saints, with countless statues carved in their image and innumerable cathedrals raised to their memories. A Jewish maiden is your ideal of motherhood and womanhood.
A Jewish rebel-prophet is the central figure in your religious worship.
We have pulled down your idols, cast aside your racial inheritance, and substituted for them our God and our traditions. No conquest in history can even remotely compare with this clean sweep of our conquest over you.

How did we do it ? Almost by accident. Two thousand years ago nearly, in far-off Palestine, our religion had fallen into decay and materialism. Money-changers were in possession of the temple.
Degenerate, selfish priests mulcted our people and grew fat. Then a young patriot-idealist arose and went about

the land calling for a revival of faith. He had no thought of setting up a new church.

Like all the prophets before him, his only aim was to purify and revitalize the old creed. He attacked the priests and drove the money-changers from the temple. This brought him into conflict with the established order and its supporting pillars.

The Roman authorities, who were in occupation of the country, fearing his revolutionary agitation as a political effort to oust them, arrested him, tried him and condemned him to death by crucifixion, a common form of execution at that time.

The followers of Jesus of Nazareth, mainly slaves and poor workmen, in their bereavement and disappointment, turned away from the world and formed themselves into a brotherhood of pacifist non-resisters, sharing the memory of their crucified leader and living together communistically. They were merely a new sect in Judea, without power or consequence, neither the first nor the last.

Only after the destruction of Jerusalem by the Romans did the new creed come into prominence.
Then a patriotic Jew named Paul or Saul conceived the idea of humbling the Roman power by destroying the morale of its soldiery with the doctrines of love and non-resistance preached by the little sect of Jewish Christians. He became the Apostle to the Gentiles, he who hitherto had been one of the most active persecutors of the band. And so well did Paul do his work that within four centuries the great empire which had subjugated Palestine along with half of the world, was a heap of ruins.
And the law which went forth from Zion became the official religion of Rome.

This was the beginning of our dominance in your world. But it was only a beginning. From this time forth your history is little more than a struggle for mastery between your own old pagan spirit and our Jewish spirit. Half your wars, great and little, are religious wars, fought over the interpretation of one thing or another in our teachings. You no sooner broke free from your primitive religious simplicity and attempted the practice of the pagan Roman learning than Luther armed with our gospels arose to down you and re-enthrone our heritage. Take the three principal revolutions in modern times — the French, the American and the Russian. What are they but the triumph of the Jewish idea of social, political and economic justice?

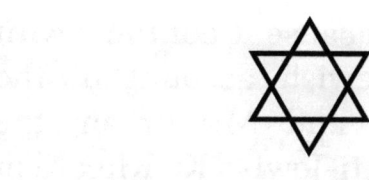

And the end is still a long way off. We still dominate you. At this very moment your churches are torn asunder by a civil war between Fundamentalists and Modernists, that is to say between those who cling to our teachings and traditions literally and those who are striving by slow steps to dispossess us.

In Dayton, Tennessee, a Bible-bred community forbids the teaching of your science because it conflicts with our ancient Jewish account of the origin of life; and Mr. Bryan, the leader of the anti-Jewish Ku Klux Klan in the Democratic National Convention, makes the supreme fight of his life in our behalf, without noticing the contradiction. Again and again the Puritan heritage of Judea breaks out in waves of stage censorship, Sunday blue laws and national prohibition acts. And while these things are happening you twaddle about Jewish influence in the movies!

Is it any wonder you resent us? We have put a clog upon your progress. We have imposed upon you an alien book and an alien faith which you cannot swallow or digest, which is at cross-purposes with your native spirit, which keeps you ever-lastingly ill-at-ease, and which you lack the spirit either to reject or to accept in full.

In full, of course, you never have accepted our Christian teachings. In your hearts you still are pagans. You still love war and graven images and strife. You still take pride in the glory of the nude human figure. Your social conscience, in spite of all democracy and all your social revolutions, is still a pitifully imperfect thing. We have merely divided your soul, confused your impulses, paralyzed your desires. In the midst of battle you are obliged to kneel down to him who commanded you to turn the other cheek, who said "Resist not evil" and "Blessed are the peacemakers."

In your lust for gain you are suddenly disturbed by a memory from your Sunday-school days about taking no thought for the morrow. In your industrial struggles, when you would smash a strike without compunction, you are suddenly reminded that the poor are blessed and that men are brothers in the Fatherhood of the Lord. And as you are about to yield to temptation, your Jewish training puts a deterrent hand on your shoulder and dashes the brimming cup from your lips. You Christians have never become Christianized. To that extent we have failed with you. But we have forever spoiled the fun of paganism for you.

So why should you not resent us? If we were in your place we should probably dislike you more cordially than you do us. But we should make no bones about telling you why. We should not resort to subterfuges and transparent pretexts. With millions of painfully respectable Jewish shopkeepers all about us we should not insult your intelligence and our own honesty by talking about communism as a Jewish philosophy. And with millions of hard-working impecunious Jewish peddlers and laborers we should not make ourselves ridiculous by talking about international capitalism as a Jewish monopoly. No, we should go straight to the point.

We should contemplate this confused, ineffectual muddle which we call civilization, this half-Christian half-pagan medley, and — were our places reversed — we should say to you point-blank : "For this mess thanks to you, to your prophets and to your Bible."

Marcus Eli Ravage
From Wikipedia

Marcus Eli Ravage (Revici) (June 25, 1884, Bârlad, Romania – October 6, 1965 Grasse, France) was a Jewish American immigrant writer who wrote many books and articles about immigration in America and Europe between the world wars.

Best known for his autobiographical book *An American in the Making* (1917), he is also known for his 1928 article, *"A Real Case Against the Jews,"* which the Third Reich German propaganda ministry and others down to the present have used as evidence that the world is dominated by Jewish conspirators.

He was also a biographer of the Rothschild family as well as of Napoleon's second wife Marie Louise.

His articles *"A real case against the Jews"* and *"Commissary to the Gentiles"*, published in the January and February 1928 issues of *Century Magazine* were translated as "a devastating admission" first in the *Czernowitz Allgemeine Zeitung* on Sept. 2, 1933.

It was then re-translated as *A voice in the wilderness; Jewish rabbi on Hitler's anti-Semitism* by Right Cause in Chicago.

WORKS

An American in the making :
The life story of an immigrant.
Harper & Brothers. 1917.

The Jew pays :
a narrative of the consequences of the war to the Jews of eastern Europe, and of the manner in which Americans have attempted to meet them.
A. A. Knopf. 1919.

The malady of Europe.
New York: Macmillan. 1923.

The story of Teapot Dome.
Republic Publishing Co. 1924.

A Real Case Against the Jews.
Century magazine. January 1928, volume 115, number 3, pages 346–350.

**The Jew
Commissary to the Gentiles :**
The First to See the Possibilities
of War by Propaganda.
*Century magazine. February 1928, volume 115,
number 4, pages 476–483.*

**Five men of Frankfort :
The story of the Rothschilds.**
L. MacVeagh - The Dial press. 1934 - 1928.

**Empress Innocence :
The life of Marie-Louise.**
New York: A.A. Knopf. 1931.

Bombshell against Christianity !
*Erfurt, Germany : U. Bodung-Verlag.
1936 - 1928.*

**Zwei Jüdische Aufsätze
vom Juden Marcus Eli Ravage :**
A Real Case Against the Jews und
Commissary to the Gentiles.
*English original text "mit deutscher Übersetzung". Erfurt, Germany : U. Bodung-Verlag.
1936, 1937, 1940, 1942.*

For more informations :

Balder Exlibris
www.balderexlibris.com

Viva Europa
www.vivaeuropa.info

Aldebaran Video
www.aldebaranvideo.tv

The Savoisien
www.the-savoisien.com

Free PDF
www.freepdf.info

PDF Archive
www.pdfarchive.info

Aryana Libris
www.aryanalibris.com

Histoire Ebook
www.histoireebook.com

Exegi monumentum aere perennius

www.ingramcontent.com/pod-product-compliance
Lightning Source LLC
LaVergne TN
LVHW041552060526
838200LV00037B/1258